This Coloring book has been designed with larger coloring areas. Let's face it.. As we reach a certain age, yes,our vision is not quite what it used to be or sometimes we just want something simple to color no matter what age we are.
As a Artist for over 40 years I find myself needing to draw and paint larger designs. Many Adult coloring books now are the small intricate designs, while Stunning when finished, coloring with the help of a magnfying glass seems to defeat the purpose of Relaxation. I have redrawn many of my original designs to add to this book in larger coloring areas. With that thought in mind, I wanted to create a coloring book that would be enjoyed by anyone wanting simpler designs to follow. I hope you enjoy this coloring book as much as I have enjoyed Creating it for you.

I have added a Test Page between each design to give protection for possible bleed through of inks or markers and as test pages to blend your colors before adding them to the coloring page if you wish.

Remember "You only have one Life, LIVE it Joyfully"

Design The Moon ART

You can also see more of my work at:
www.zazzle.com/designthemoon/products

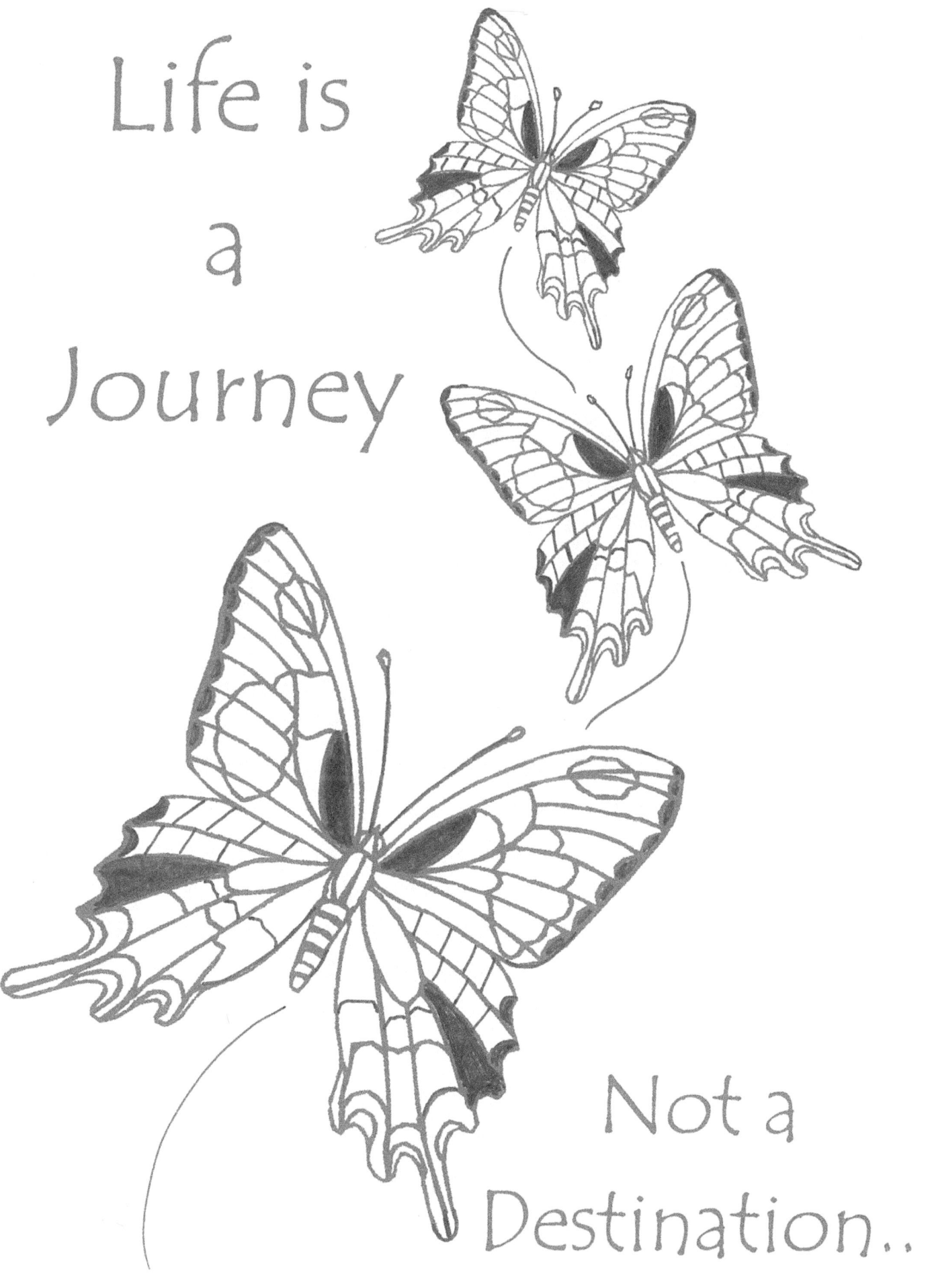

Life is
a
Journey

Not a
Destination..

This page is a TEST or Doodle Page where you can Test and blend your colors before adding them to your coloring page. It also gives protection for any possible bleedthrough of pens, paints or markers.

Notes:

_____

_____

_____

_____

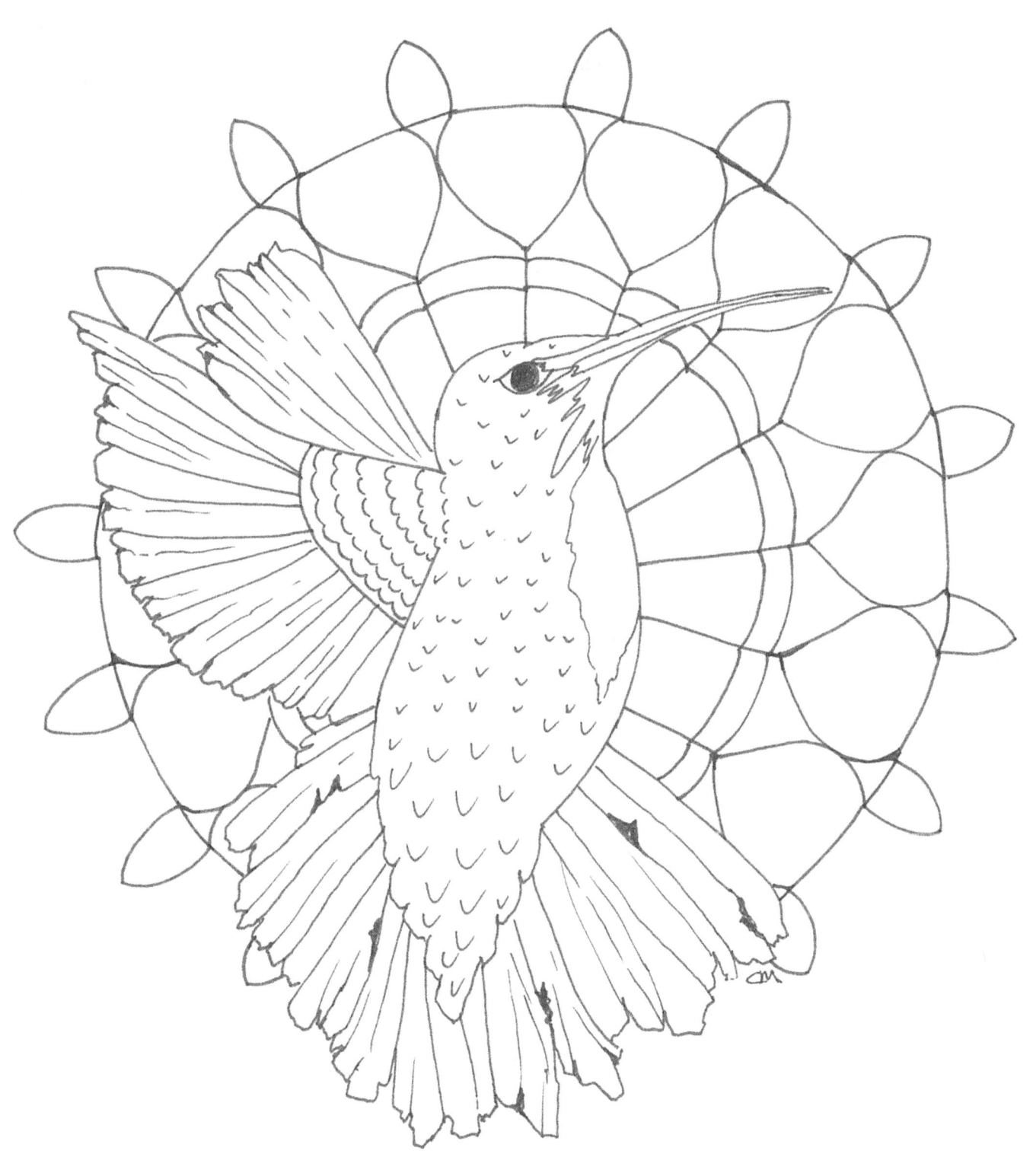

Believe that you can
and you WILL...

This page is a TEST or Doodle Page where you can Test and blend your colors before adding them to your coloring page. It also gives protection for any possible bleedthrough of pens, paints or markers.

Notes:

_____

_____

_____

_____

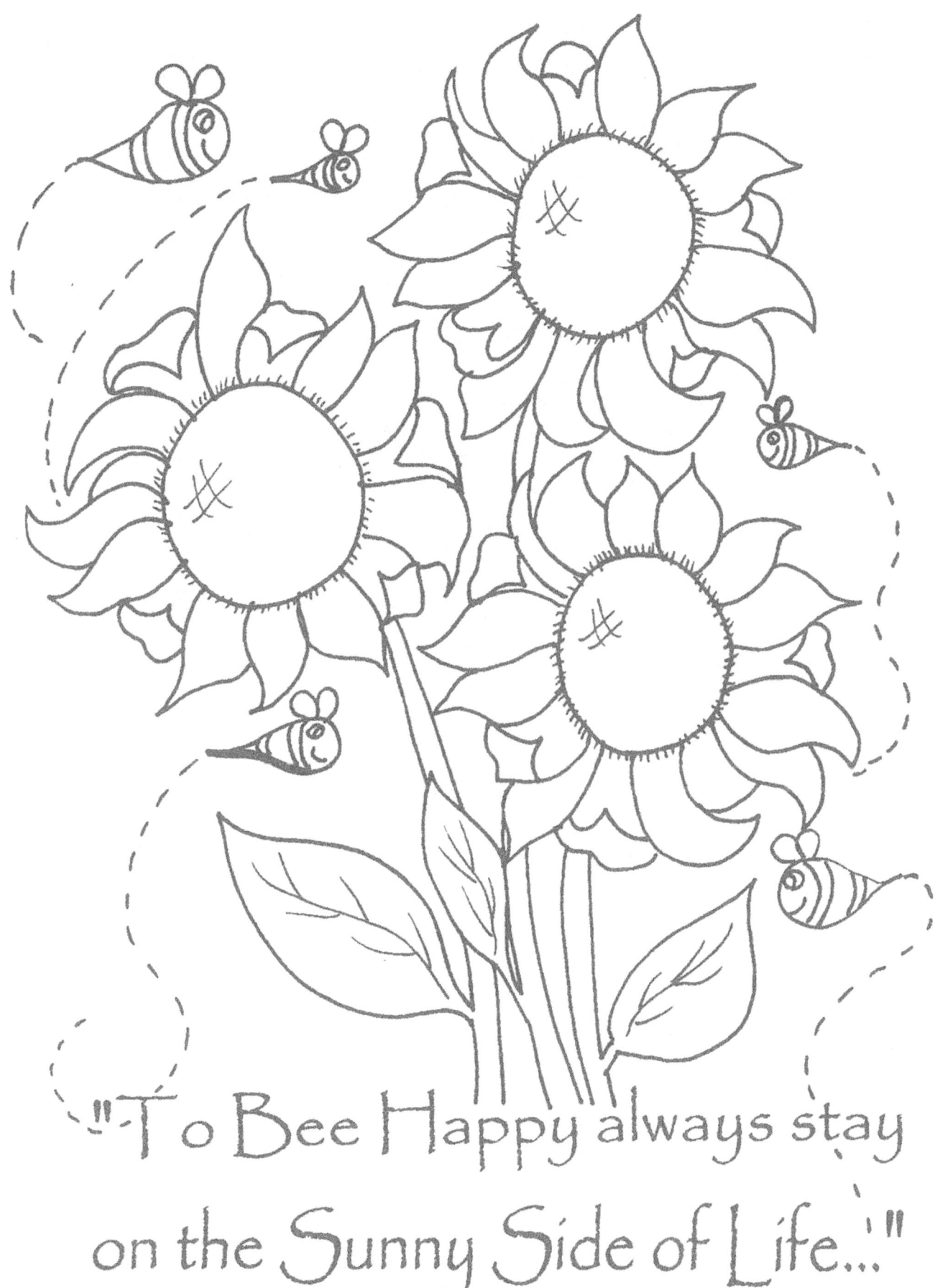

"To Bee Happy always stay
on the Sunny Side of Life..."

This page is a TEST or Doodle Page where you can Test and blend your colors before adding them to your coloring page. It also gives protection for any possible bleedthrough of pens, paints or markers.

Notes:

_____

_____

_____

_____

Some days are just

prickley....

This page is a TEST or Doodle Page where you can Test and blend your colors before adding them to your coloring page. It also gives protection for any possible bleedthrough of pens, paints or markers.

Notes:

_____

_____

_____

_____

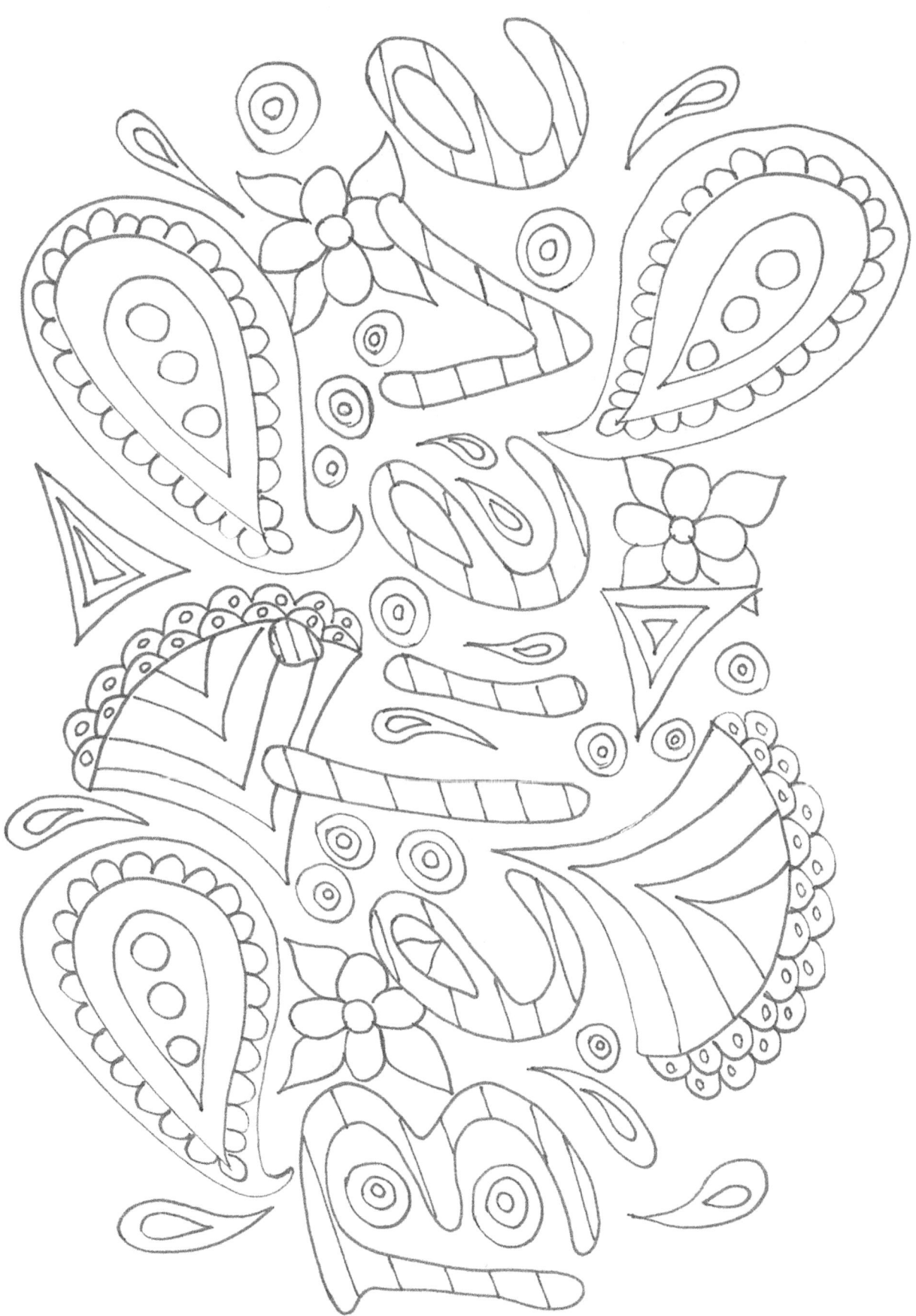

This page is a TEST or Doodle Page where you can Test and blend your colors before adding them to your coloring page. It also gives protection for any possible bleedthrough of pens, paints or markers.

Notes:

_____

_____

_____

_____

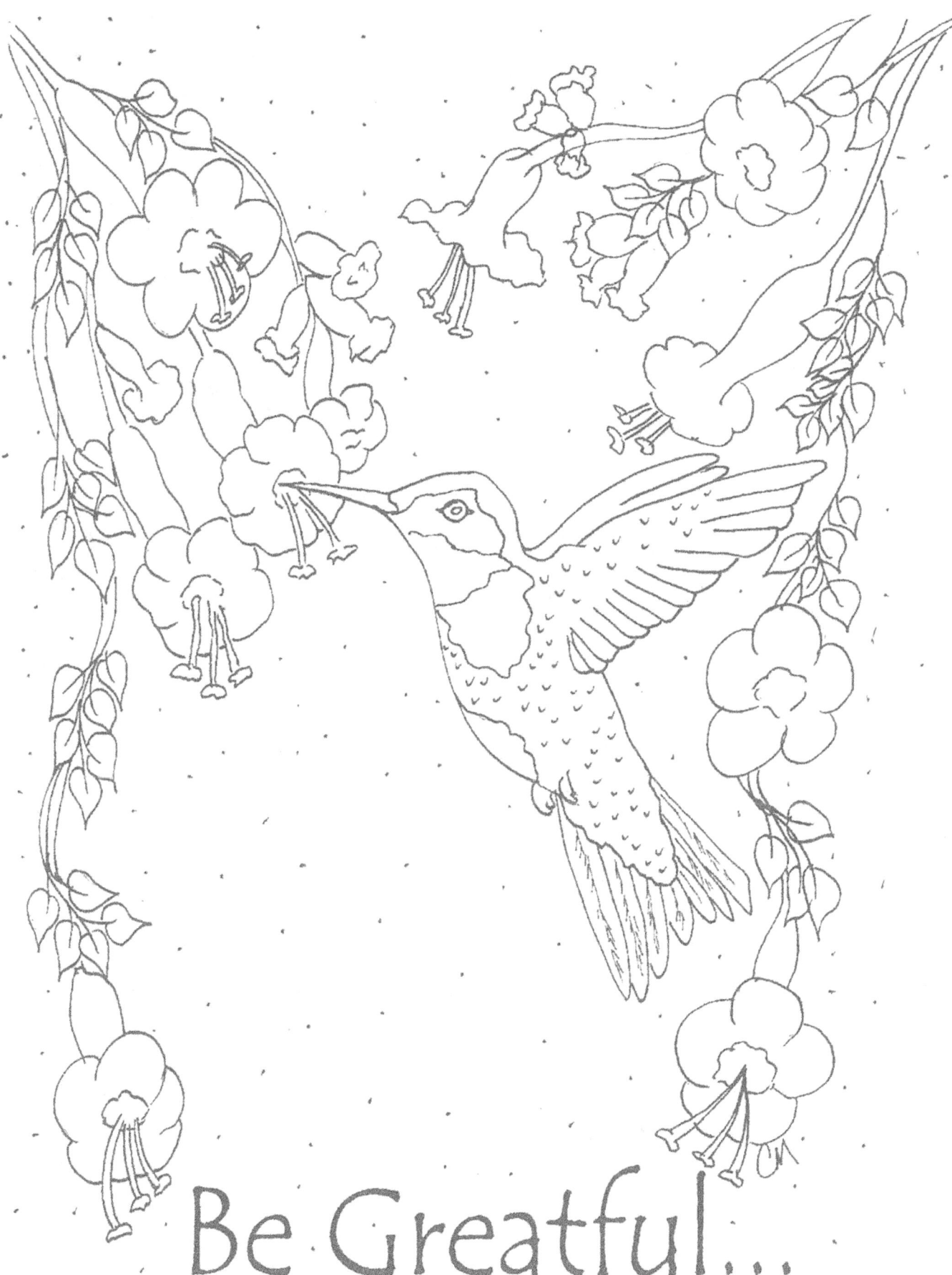

Be Greatful....

This page is a TEST or Doodle Page where you can Test and blend your colors before adding them to your coloring page. It also gives protection for any possible bleedthrough of pens, paints or markers.

Notes:

_____

_____

_____

_____

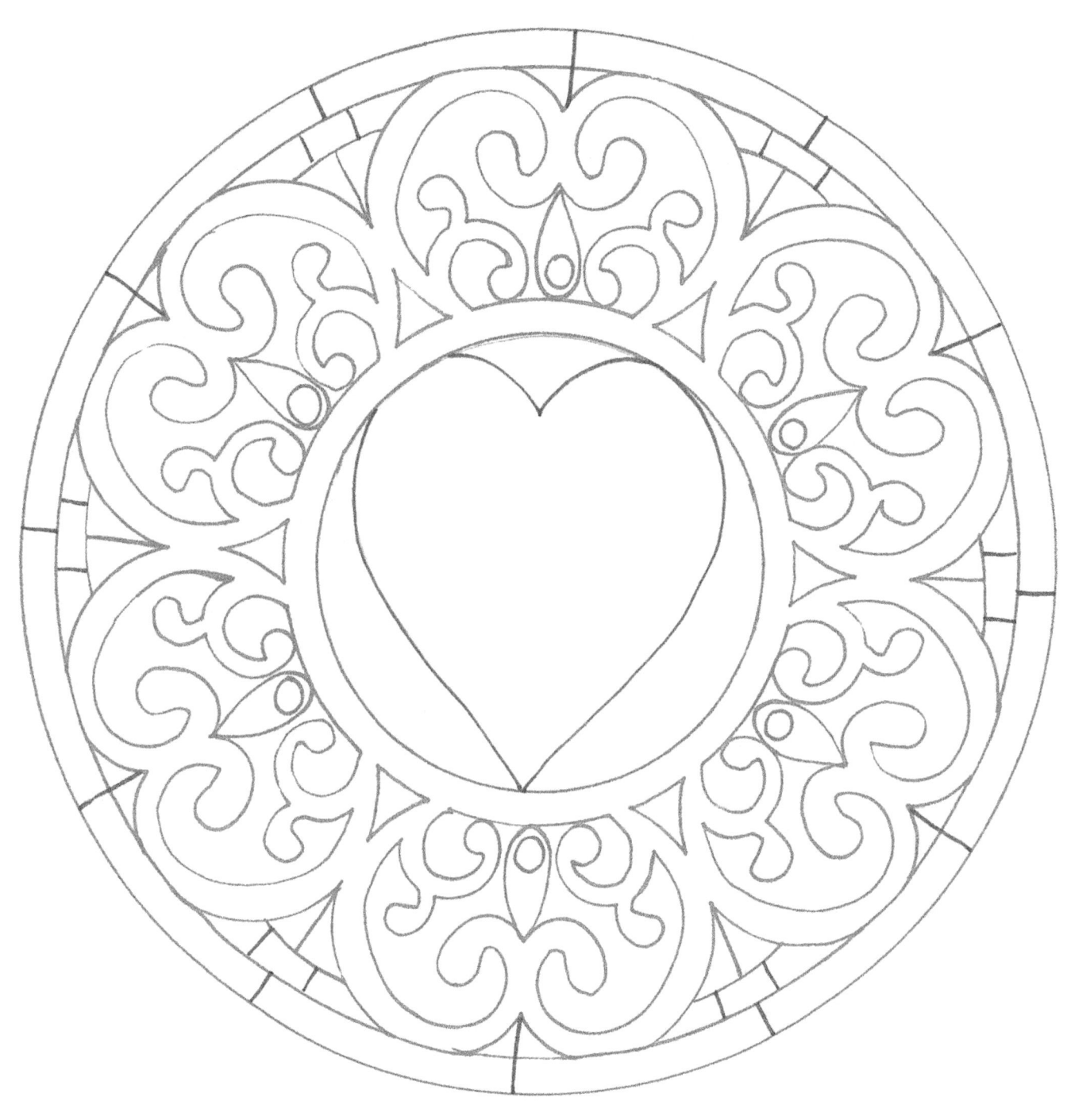

LOVE

is the Key to a Happy Life...

This page is a TEST or Doodle Page where you can Test and blend your colors before adding them to your coloring page. It also gives protection for any possible bleedthrough of pens, paints or markers.

Notes:

_____

_____

_____

_____

If the Shoe Fits...

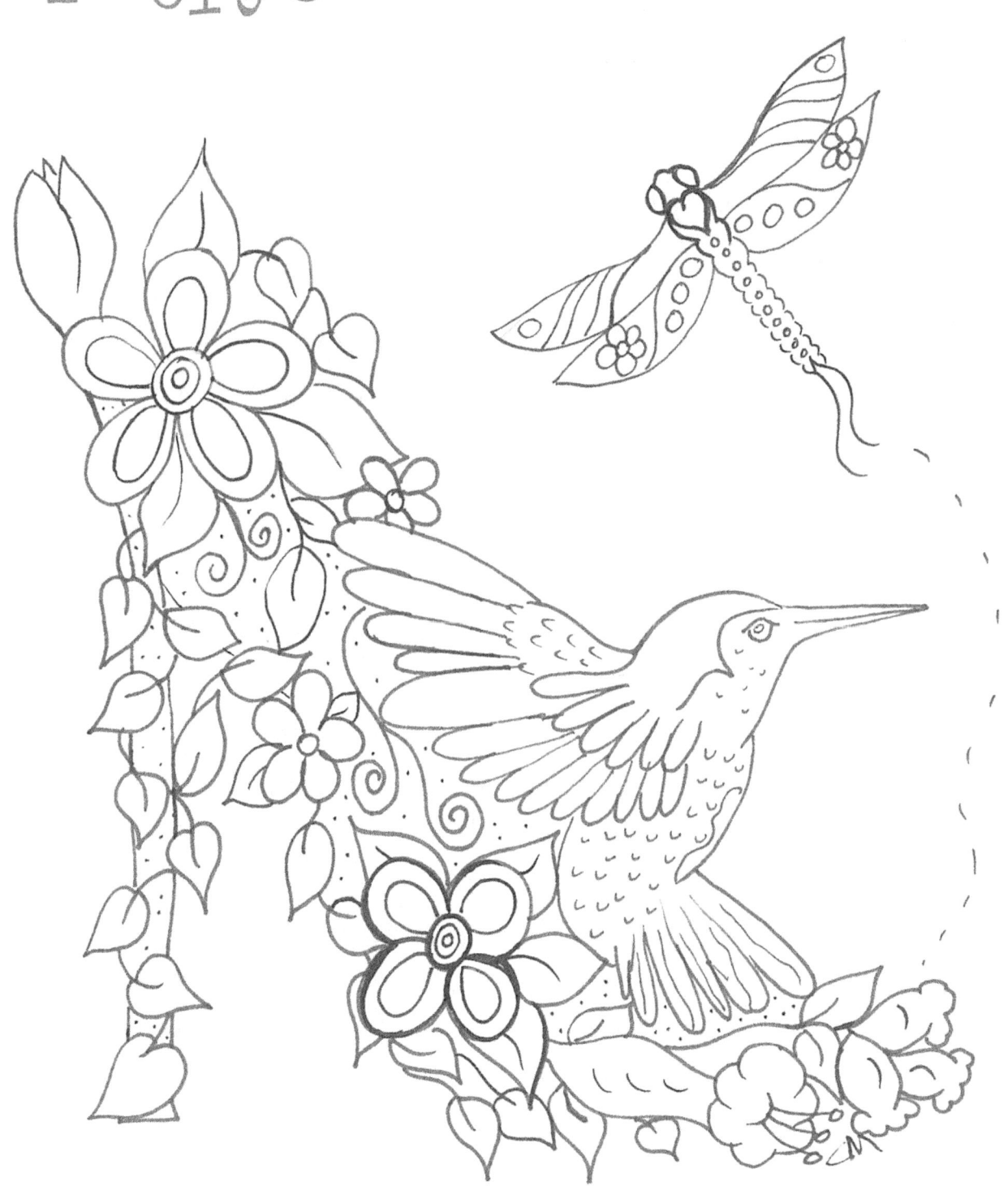

This page is a TEST or Doodle Page where you can Test and blend your colors before adding them to your coloring page. It also gives protection for any possible bleedthrough of pens, paints or markers.

Notes:

_____

_____

_____

_____

Listen to the quiet beauty

of Nature...

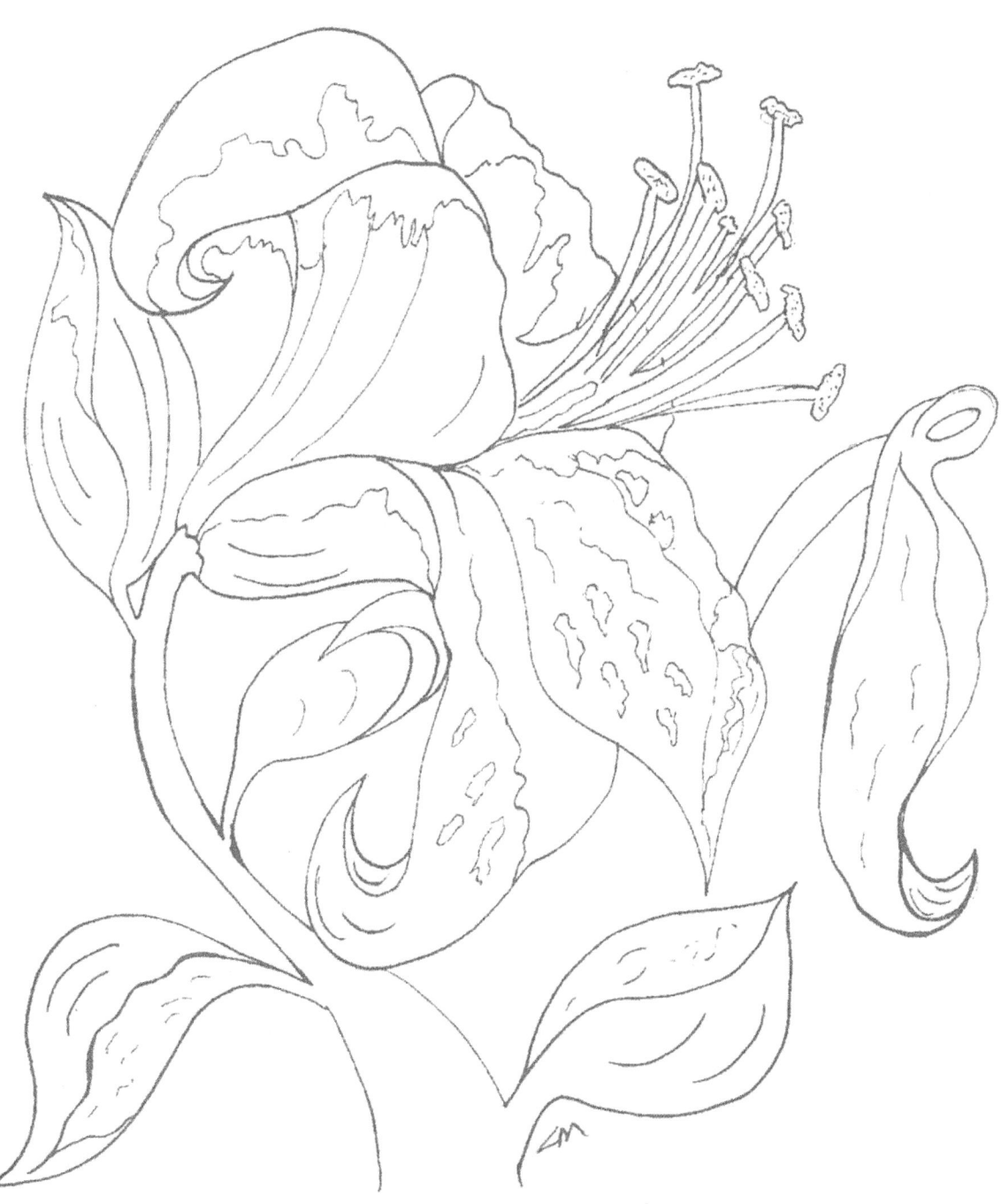

This page is a TEST or Doodle Page where you can Test and blend your colors before adding them to your coloring page. It also gives protection for any possible bleedthrough of pens, paints or markers.

Notes:

_____

_____

_____

_____

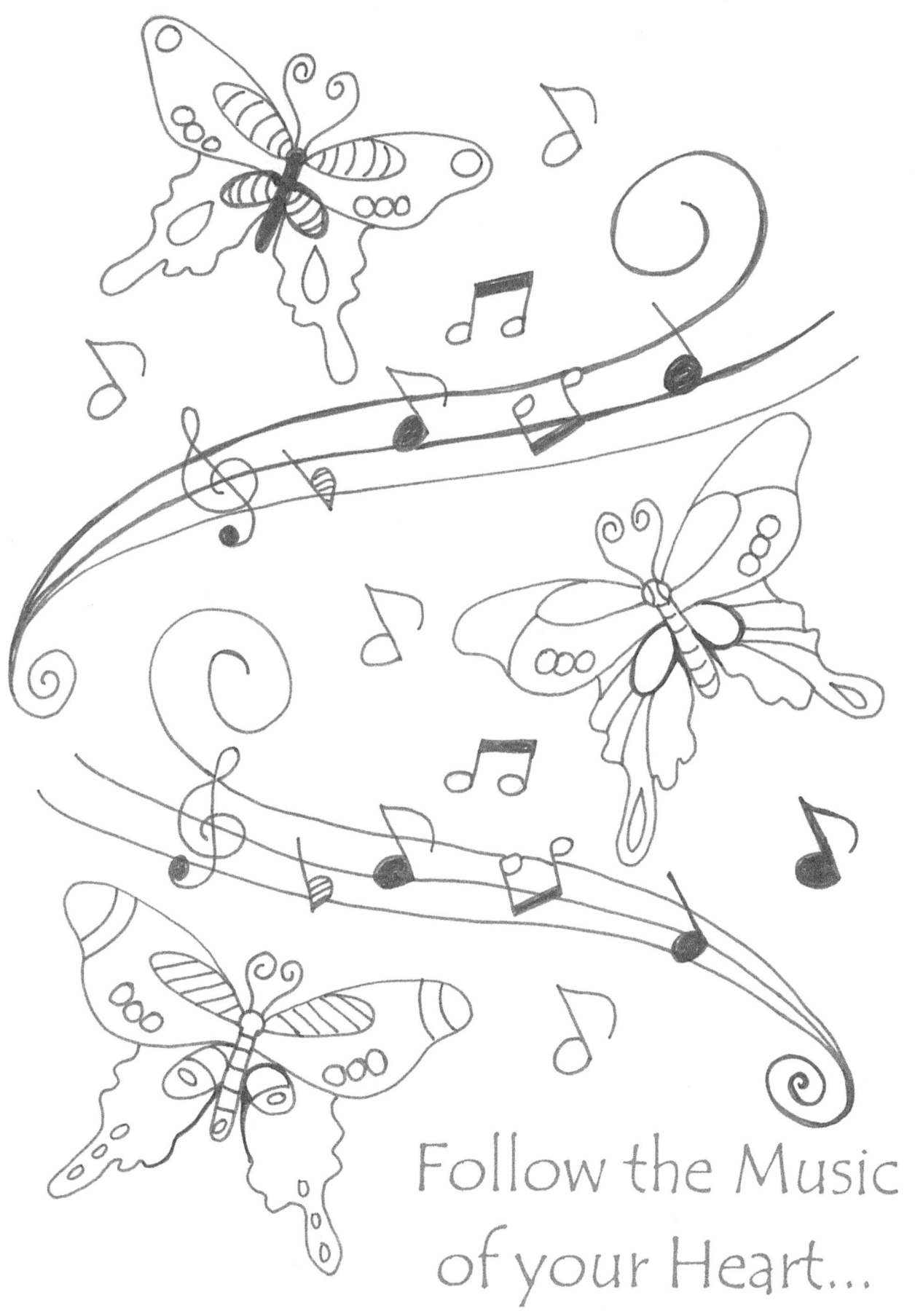

Follow the Music
of your Heart...

This page is a TEST or Doodle Page where you can Test and blend your colors before adding them to your coloring page. It also gives protection for any possible bleedthrough of pens, paints or markers.

Notes:

_____

_____

_____

_____

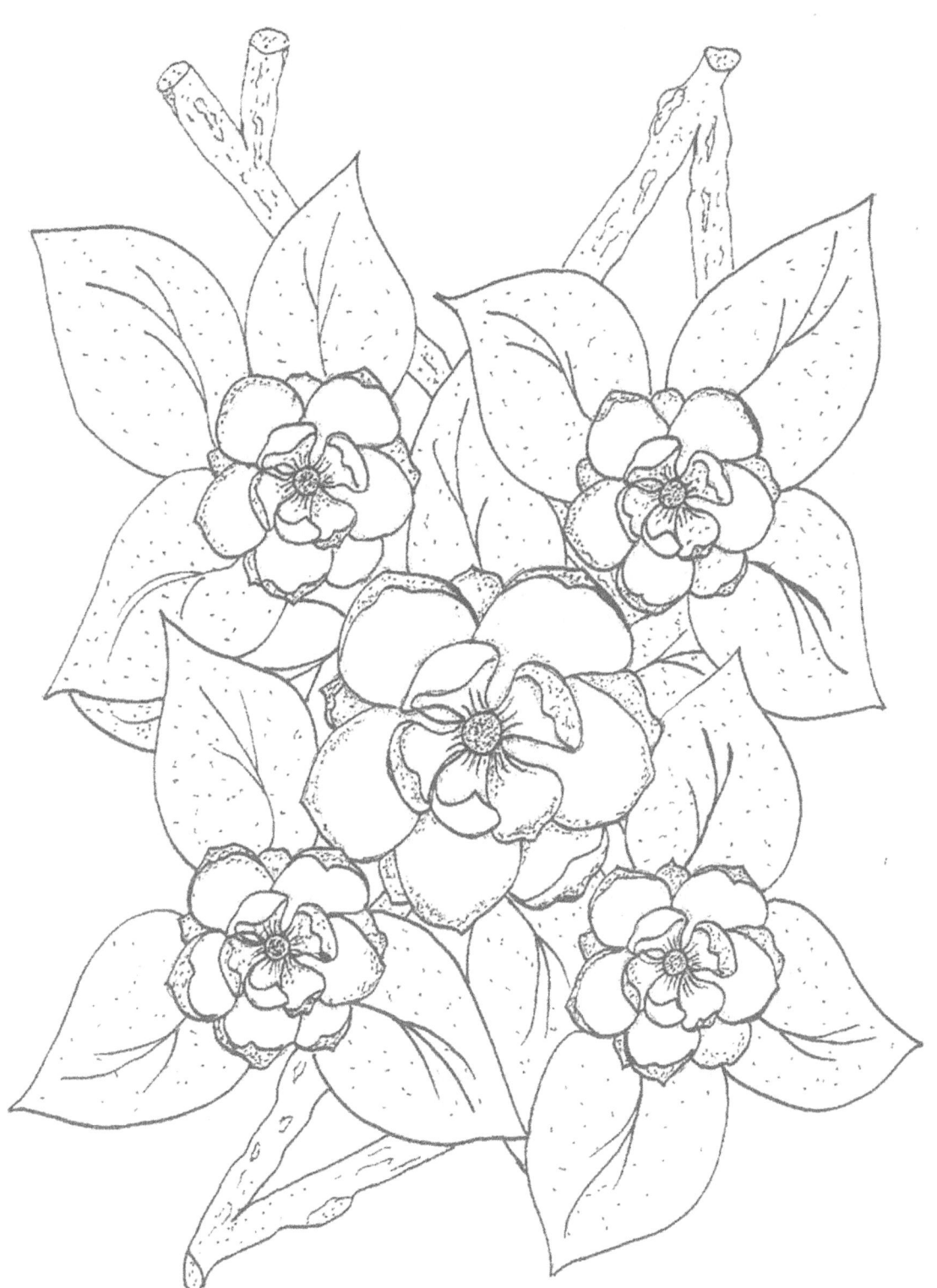

*Life is Better when we focus
on what Truly Matters....*

This page is a TEST or Doodle Page where you can Test and blend your colors before adding them to your coloring page. It also gives protection for any possible bleedthrough of pens, paints or markers.

Notes:

_____

_____

_____

_____

The Cardinal knows

ALL your

Hopes and Dreams..

This page is a TEST or Doodle Page where you can Test and blend your colors before adding them to your coloring page. It also gives protection for any possible bleedthrough of pens, paints or markers.

Notes:

_____

_____

_____

_____

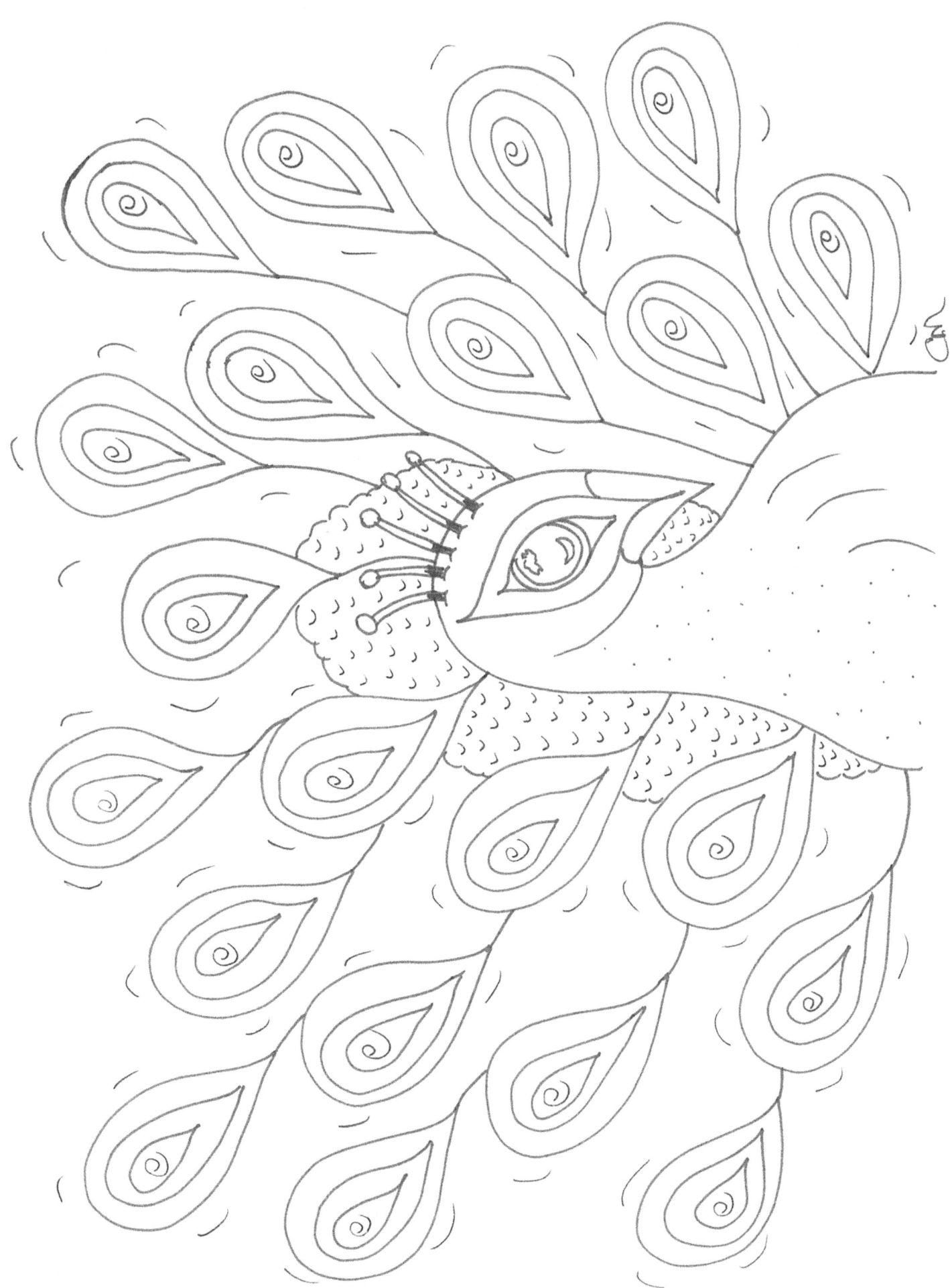

This page is a TEST or Doodle Page where you can Test and blend your colors before adding them to your coloring page. It also gives protection for any possible bleedthrough of pens, paints or markers.

Notes:

_____

_____

_____

_____

Sometimes life doesn't give

you what you Want..

because you deserve More...

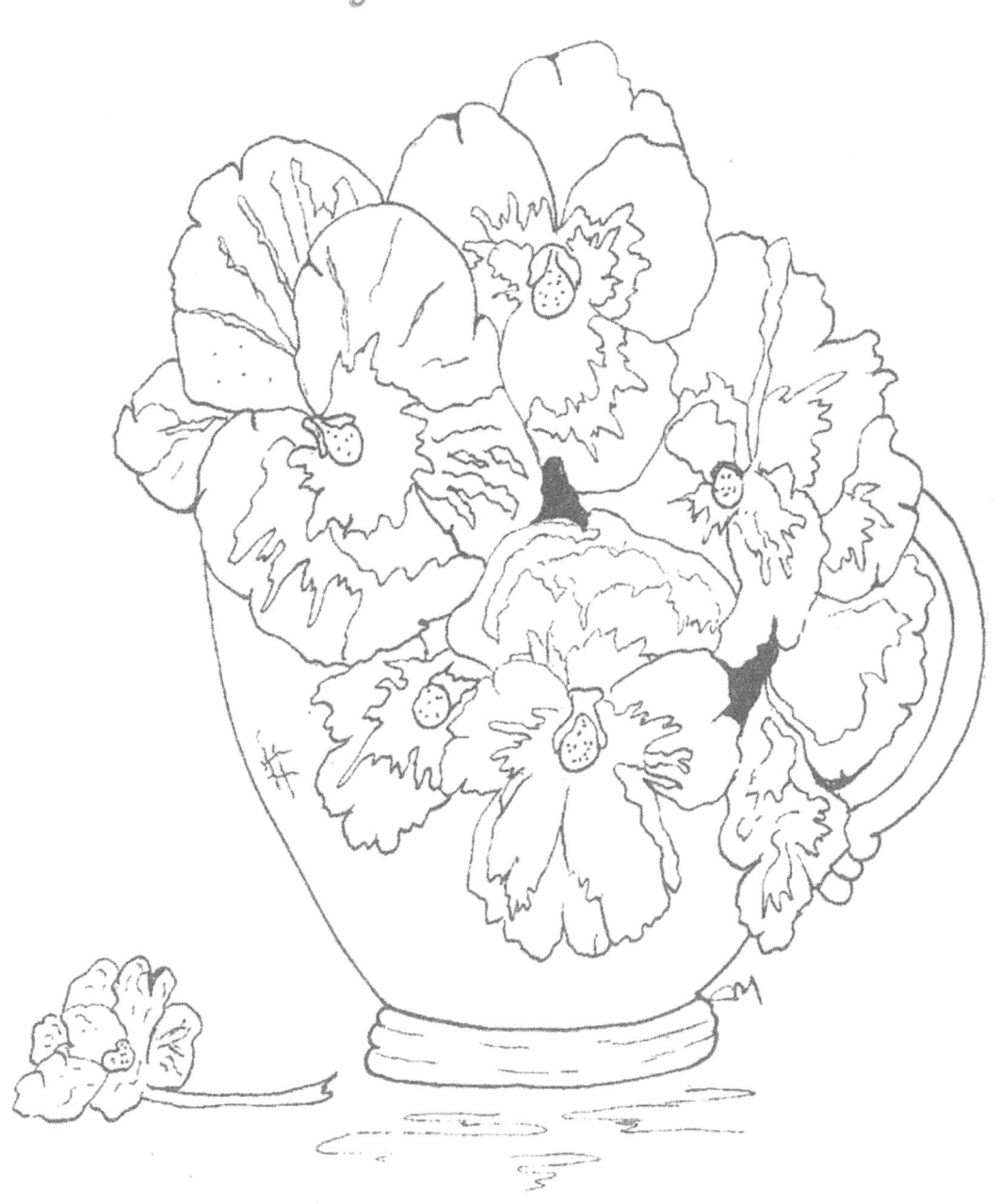

This page is a TEST or Doodle Page where you can Test and blend your colors before adding them to your coloring page. It also gives protection for any possible bleedthrough of pens, paints or markers.

Notes:

_____

_____

_____

_____

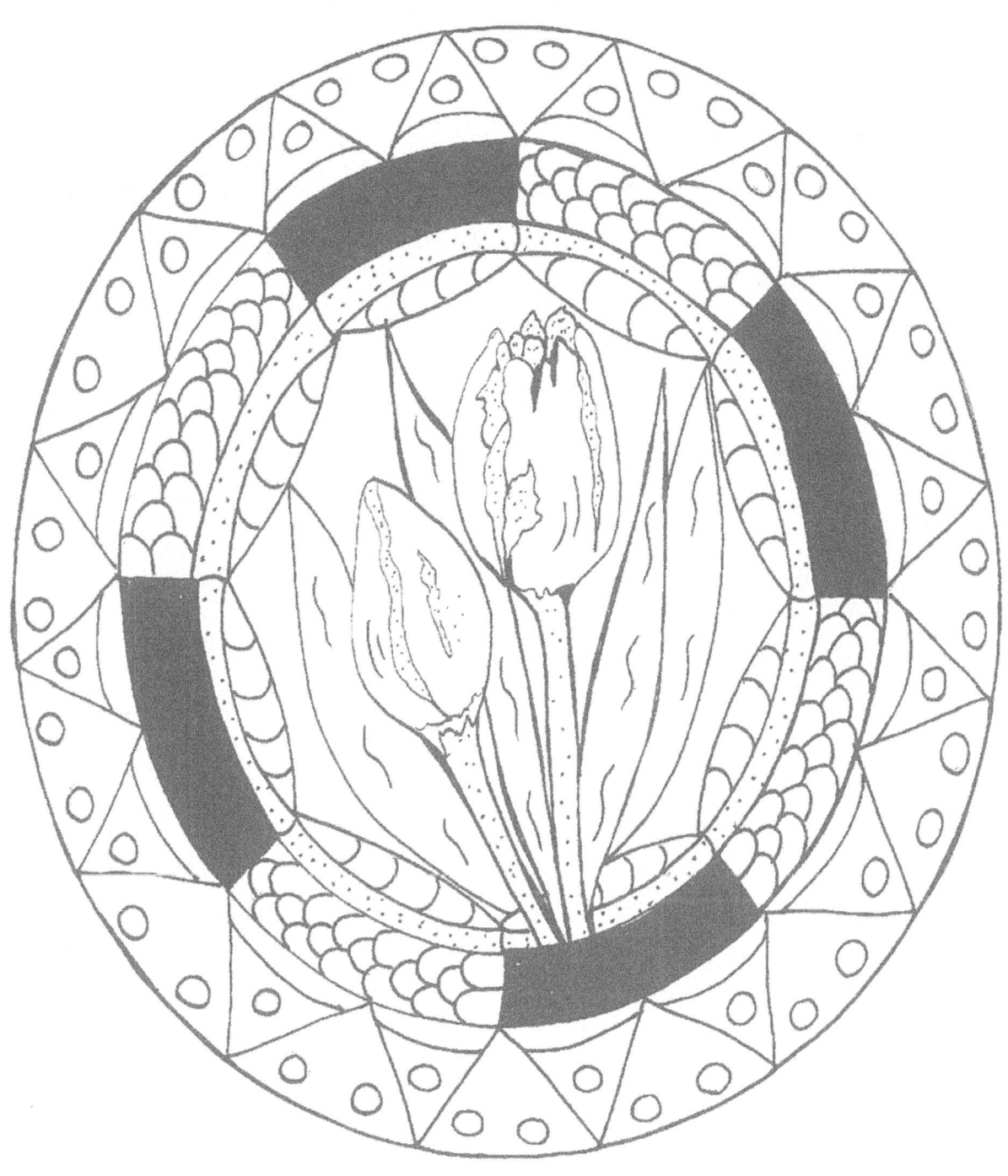

You are confined only by
the walls you build yourself..

This page is a TEST or Doodle Page where you can Test and blend your colors before adding them to your coloring page. It also gives protection for any possible bleedthrough of pens, paints or markers.

Notes:

_____

_____

_____

_____

_____

Always Dance to your Own Music....

This page is a TEST or Doodle Page where you can Test and blend your colors before adding them to your coloring page. It also gives protection for any possible bleedthrough of pens, paints or markers.

Notes:

_____

_____

_____

_____

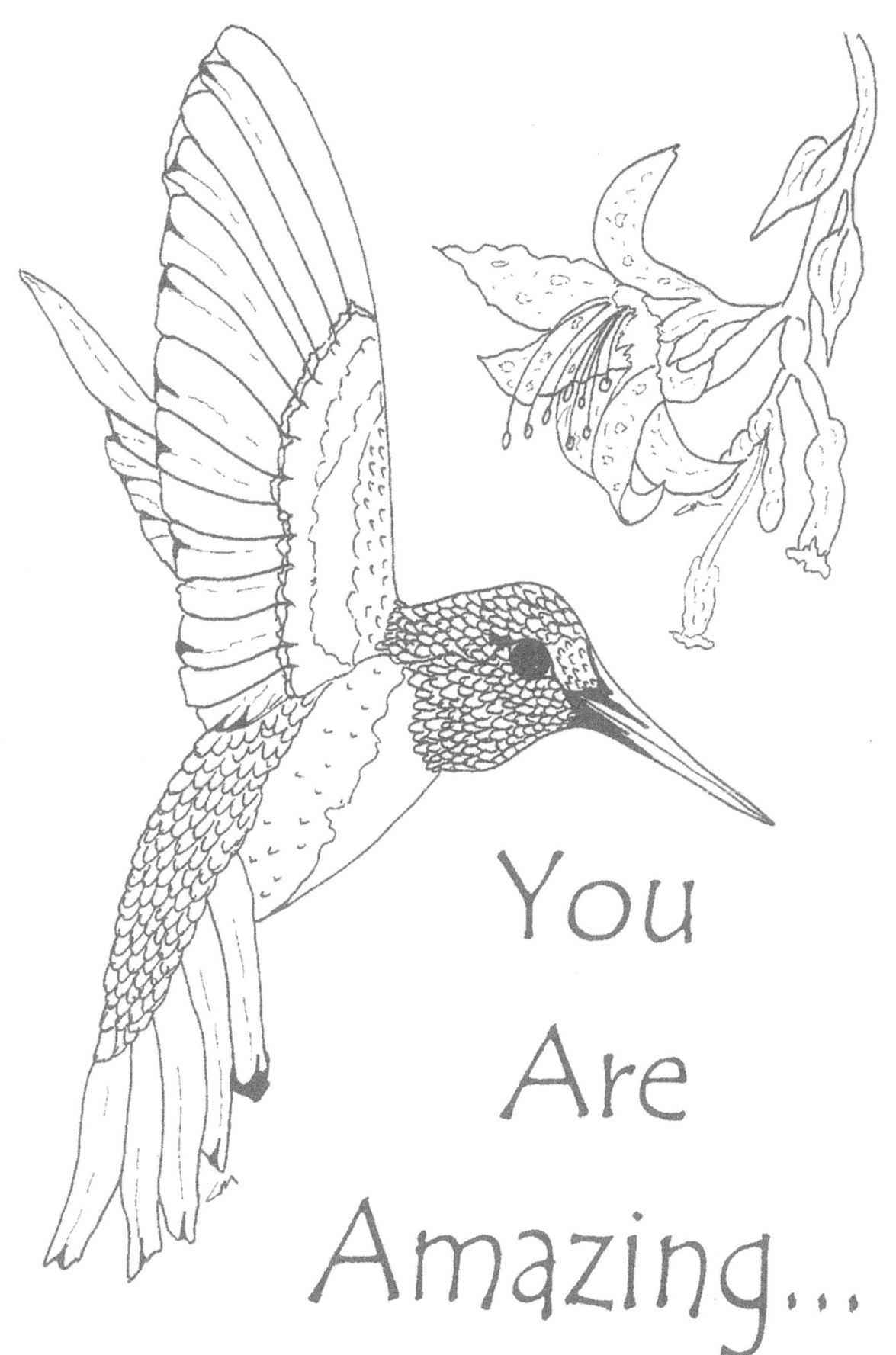

You
Are
Amazing....

This page is a TEST or Doodle Page where you can Test and blend your colors before adding them to your coloring page. It also gives protection for any possible bleedthrough of pens, paints or markers.

Notes:

_____

_____

_____

_____

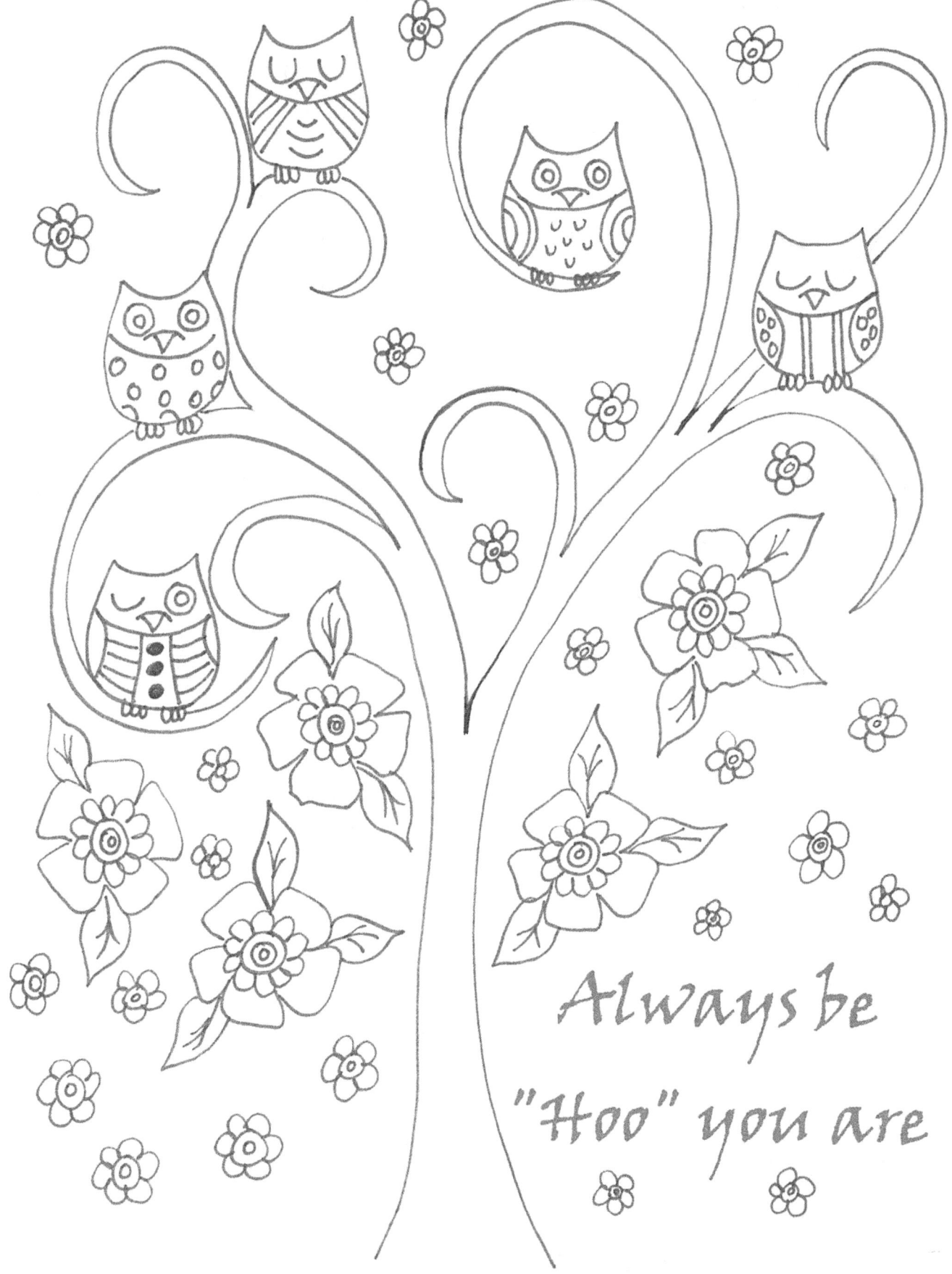

This page is a TEST or Doodle Page where you can Test and blend your colors before adding them to your coloring page. It also gives protection for any possible bleedthrough of pens, paints or markers.

Notes:

_____

_____

_____

_____

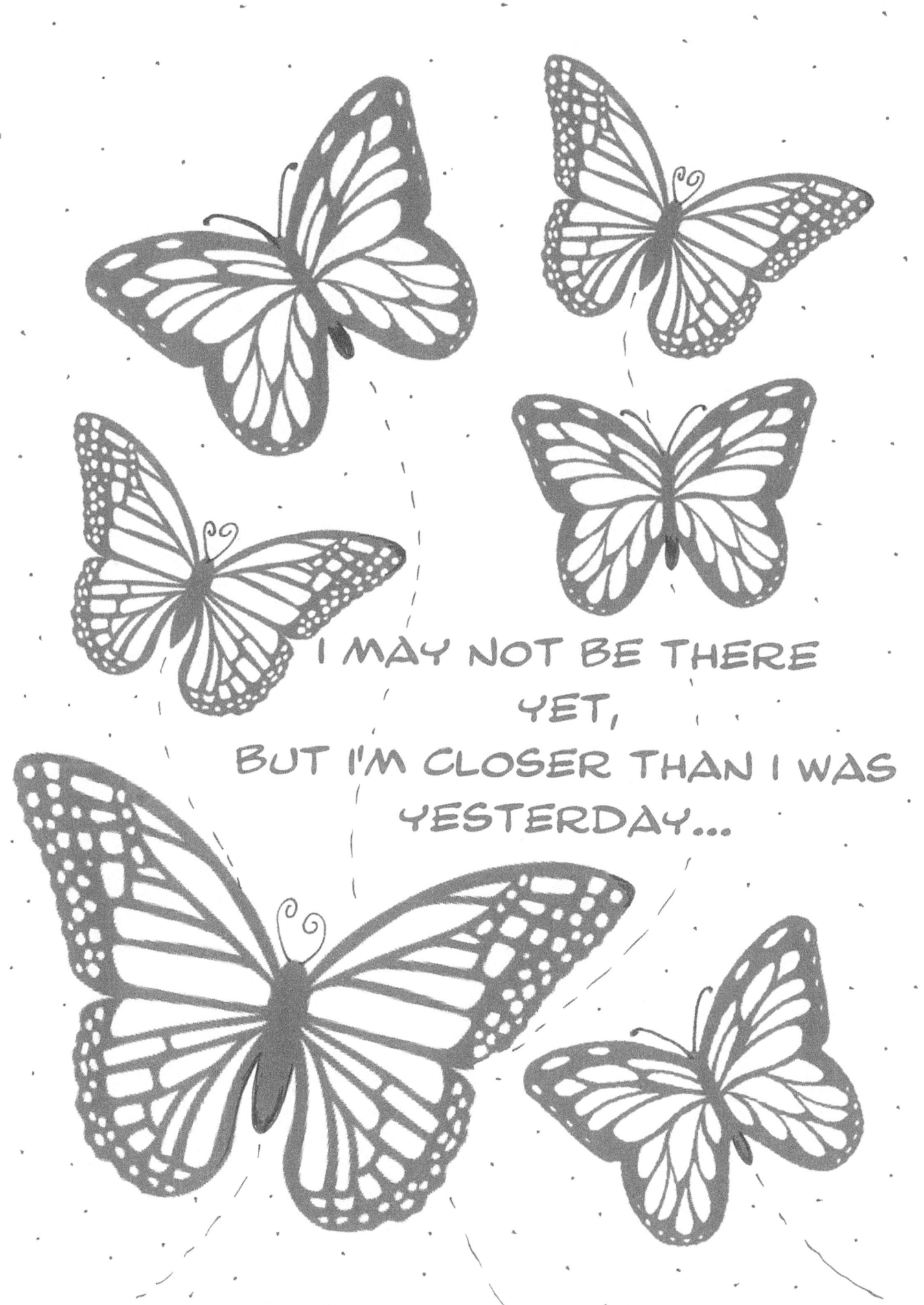

This page is a TEST or Doodle Page where you can Test and blend your colors before adding them to your coloring page. It also gives protection for any possible bleedthrough of pens, paints or markers.

Notes:

_____

_____

_____

_____

_____

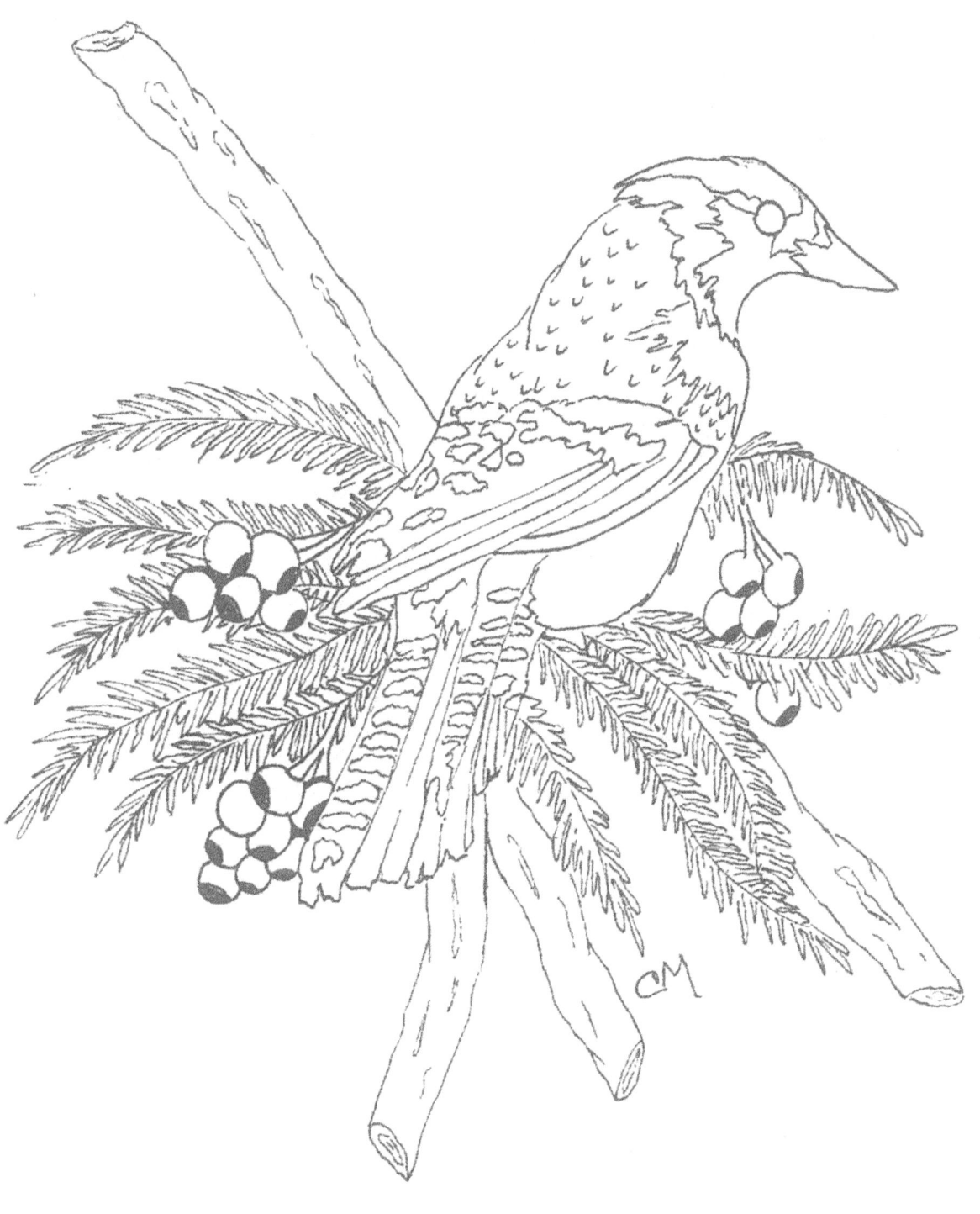

May the Bluebird of Happiness
Always live in your Heart...

This page is a TEST or Doodle Page where you can Test and blend your colors before adding them to your coloring page. It also gives protection for any possible bleedthrough of pens, paints or markers.

Notes:

_____

_____

_____

_____

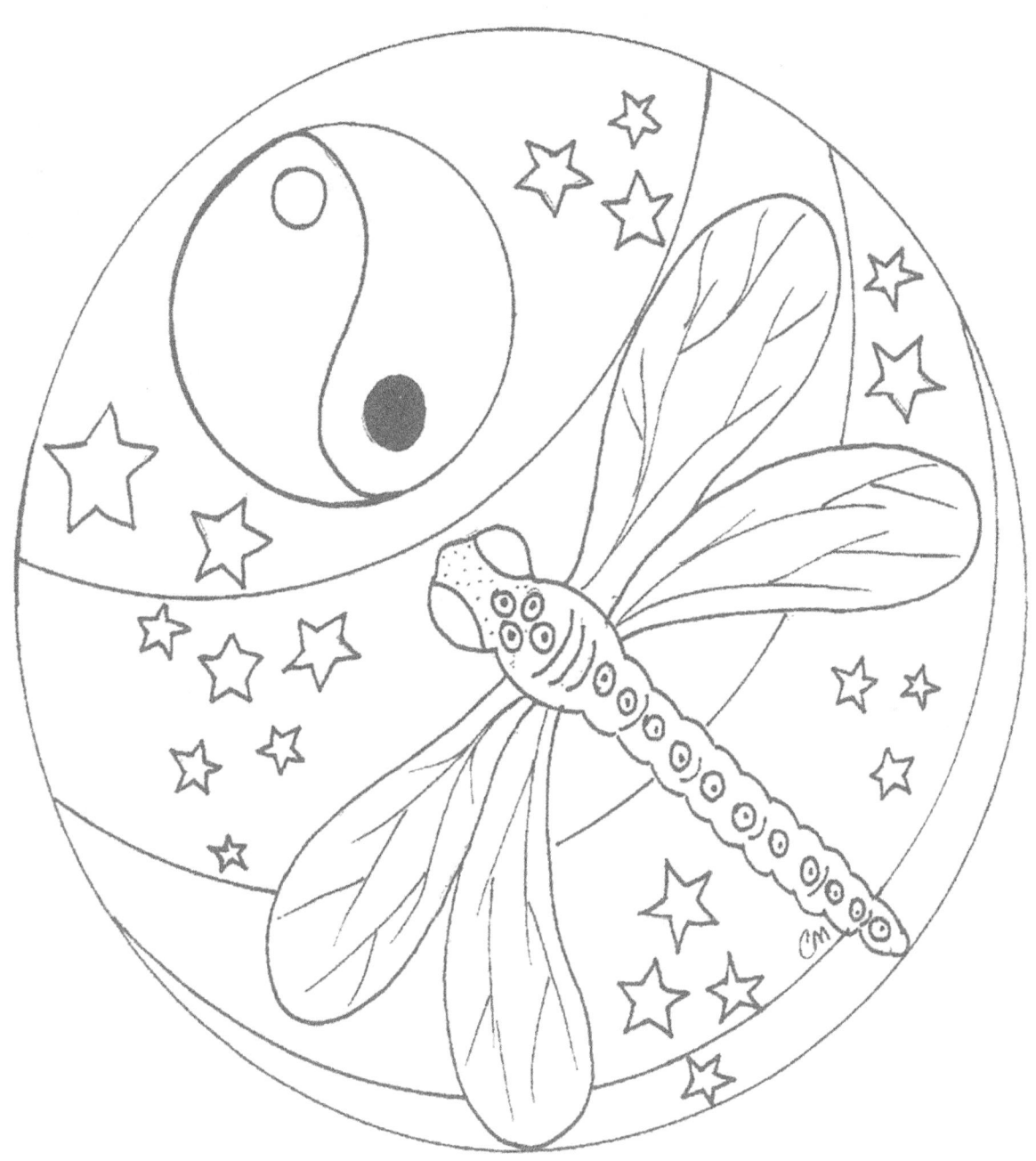

STARS CAN'T
SHINE WITHOUT
DARKNESS..

This page is a TEST or Doodle Page where you can Test and blend your colors before adding them to your coloring page. It also gives protection for any possible bleedthrough of pens, paints or markers.

Notes:

_____

_____

_____

_____

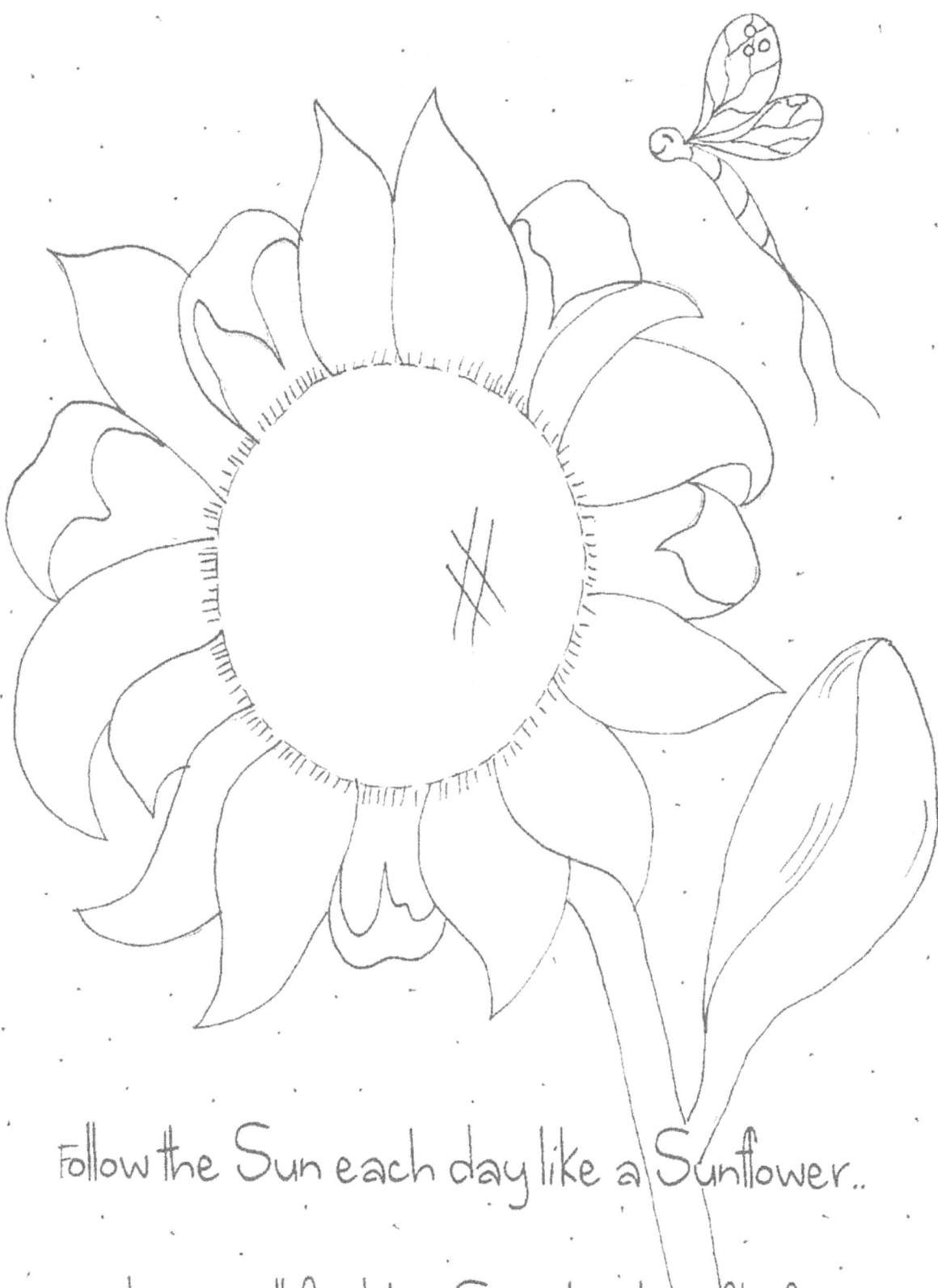

Follow the Sun each day like a Sunflower..

and you will find the Simple Joy of Life...

This page is a TEST or Doodle Page where you can Test and blend your colors before adding them to your coloring page. It also gives protection for any possible bleedthrough of pens, paints or markers.

Notes:

_____

_____

_____

_____

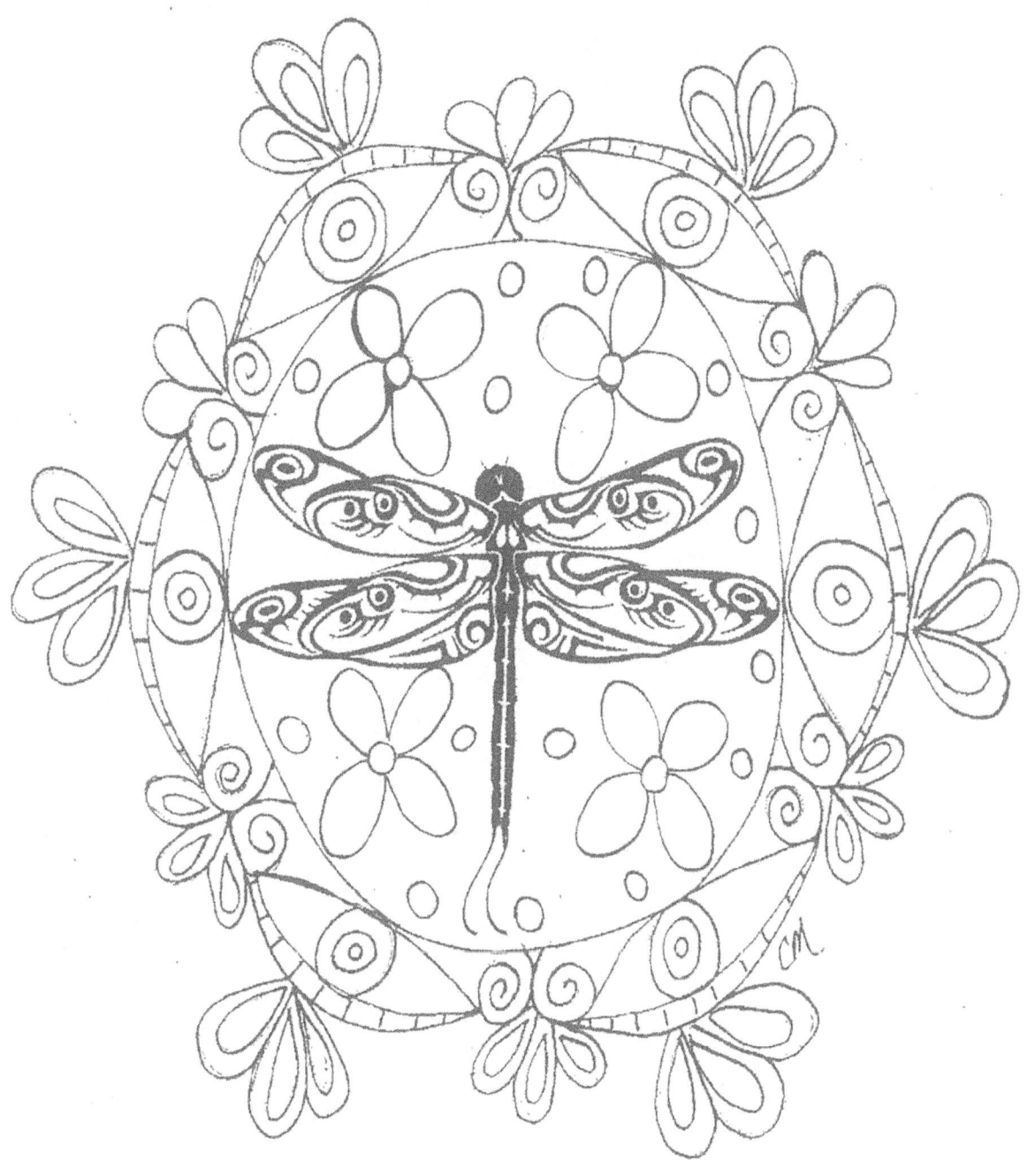

Your mind is like a Garden,

Your thoughts are like the seeds,

You can choose to grow Flowers or choose to grow

Weeds...

This page is a TEST or Doodle Page where you can Test and blend your colors before adding them to your coloring page. It also gives protection for any possible bleedthrough of pens, paints or markers.

Notes:

_____

_____

_____

_____

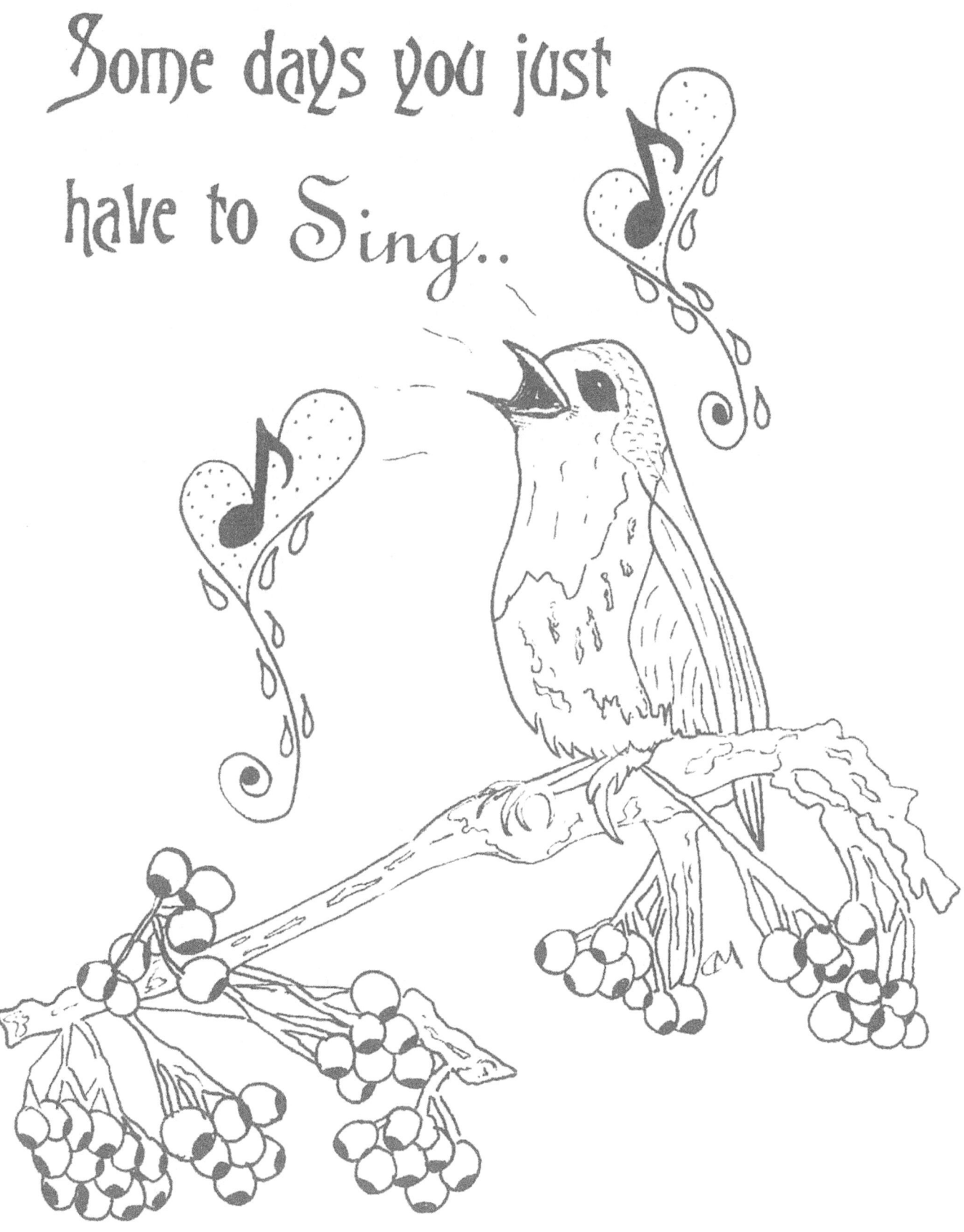

This page is a TEST or Doodle Page where you can Test and blend your colors before adding them to your coloring page. It also gives protection for any possible bleedthrough of pens, paints or markers.

Notes:

_____

_____

_____

_____

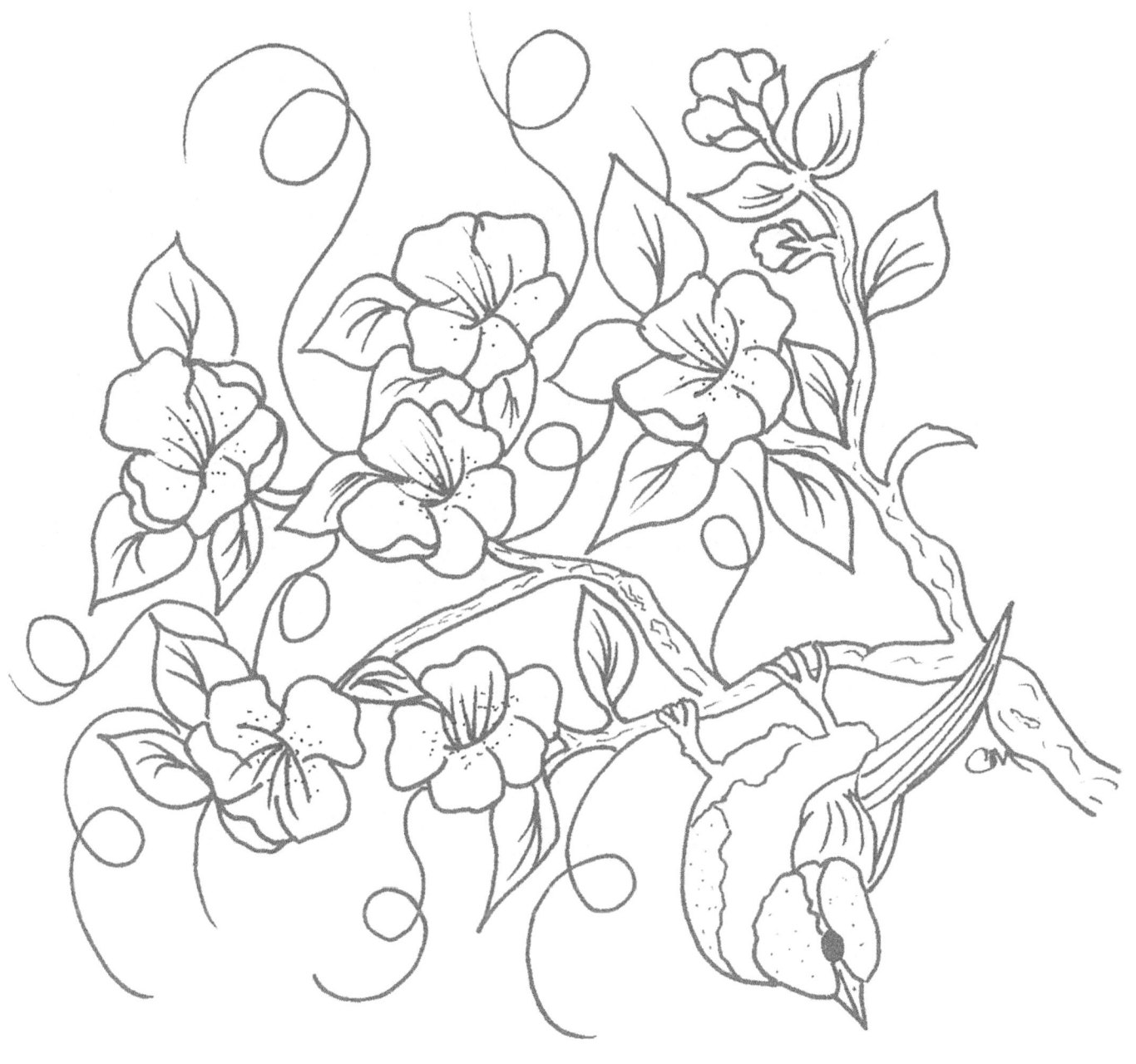

LIFE IS TOO SHORT
TO FOLLOW THE
RULES...

This page is a TEST or Doodle Page where you can Test and blend your colors before adding them to your coloring page. It also gives protection for any possible bleedthrough of pens, paints or markers.

Notes:

_____

_____

_____

_____

Life is Beautiful...

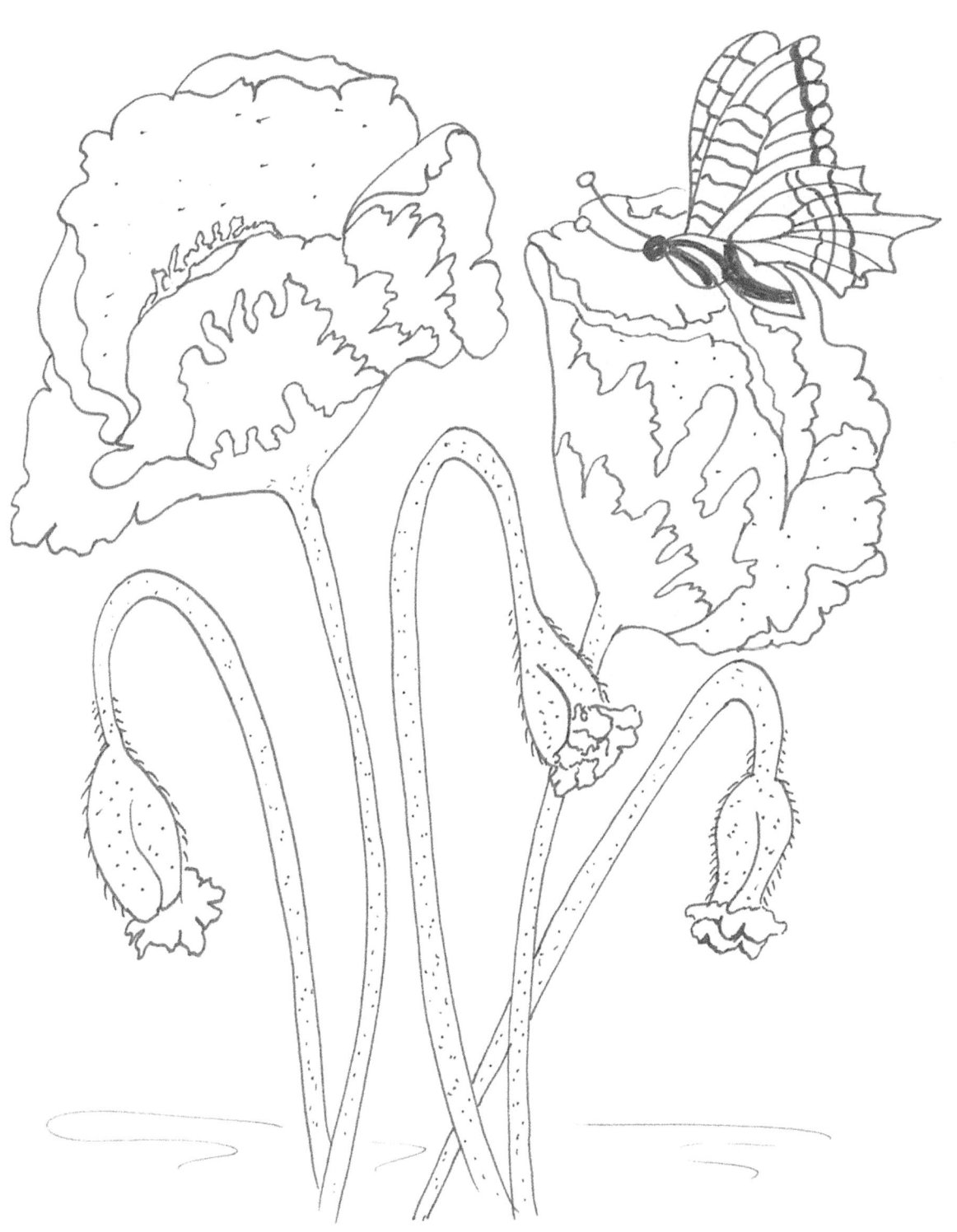

This page is a TEST or Doodle Page where you can Test and blend your colors before adding them to your coloring page. It also gives protection for any possible bleedthrough of pens, paints or markers.

Notes:

_____

_____

_____

_____

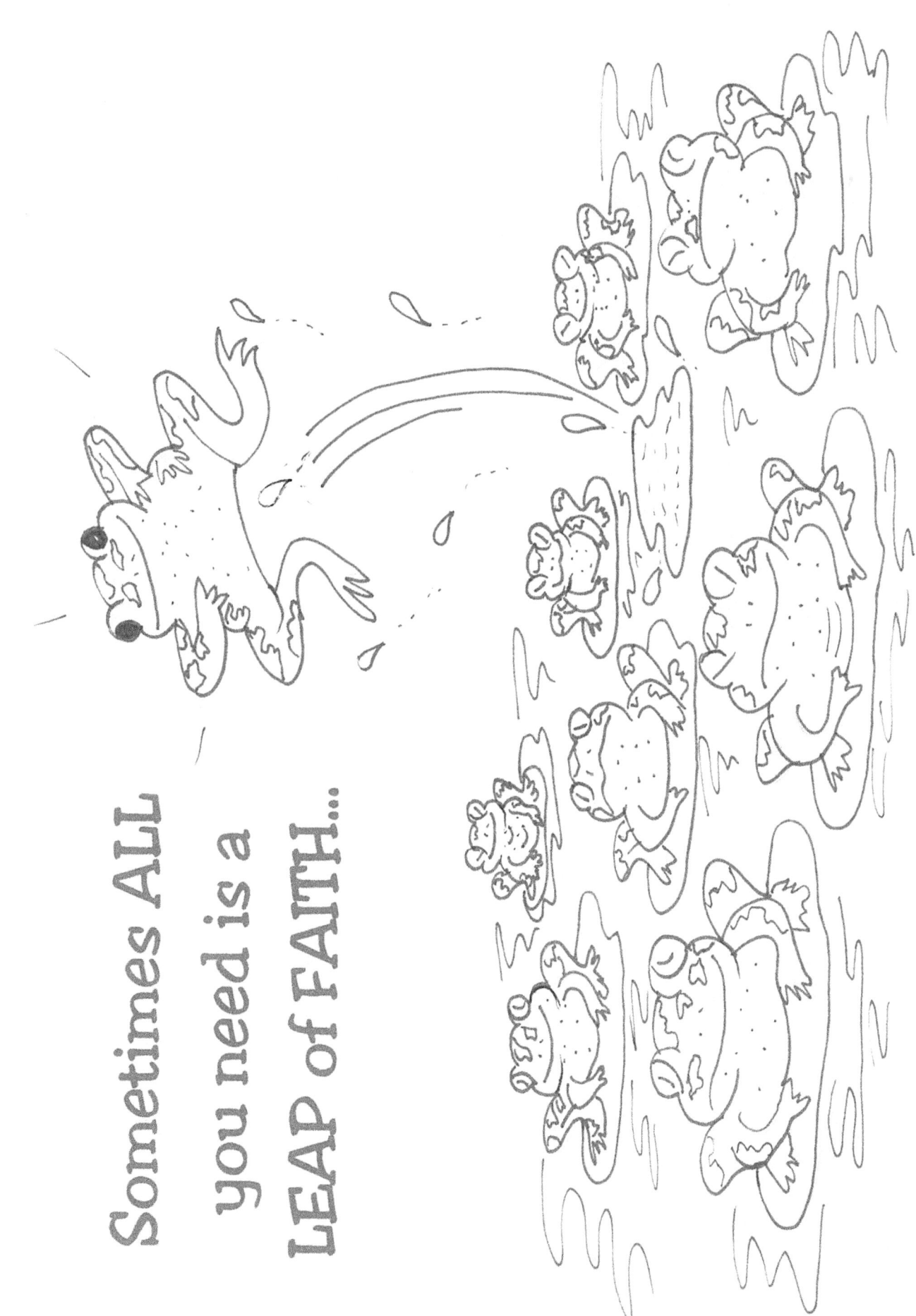

Sometimes ALL you need is a LEAP of FAITH...

This page is a TEST or Doodle Page where you can Test and blend your colors before adding them to your coloring page. It also gives protection for any possible bleedthrough of pens, paints or markers.

Notes:

_____

_____

_____

_____

This page is a TEST or Doodle Page where you can Test and blend your colors before adding them to your coloring page. It also gives protection for any possible bleedthrough of pens, paints or markers.

Notes:

_____

_____

_____

_____

Some people Feel the
Rain...
Others just get Wet...

This page is a TEST or Doodle Page where you can Test and blend your colors before adding them to your coloring page. It also gives protection for any possible bleedthrough of pens, paints or markers.

Notes:

_____

_____

_____

_____

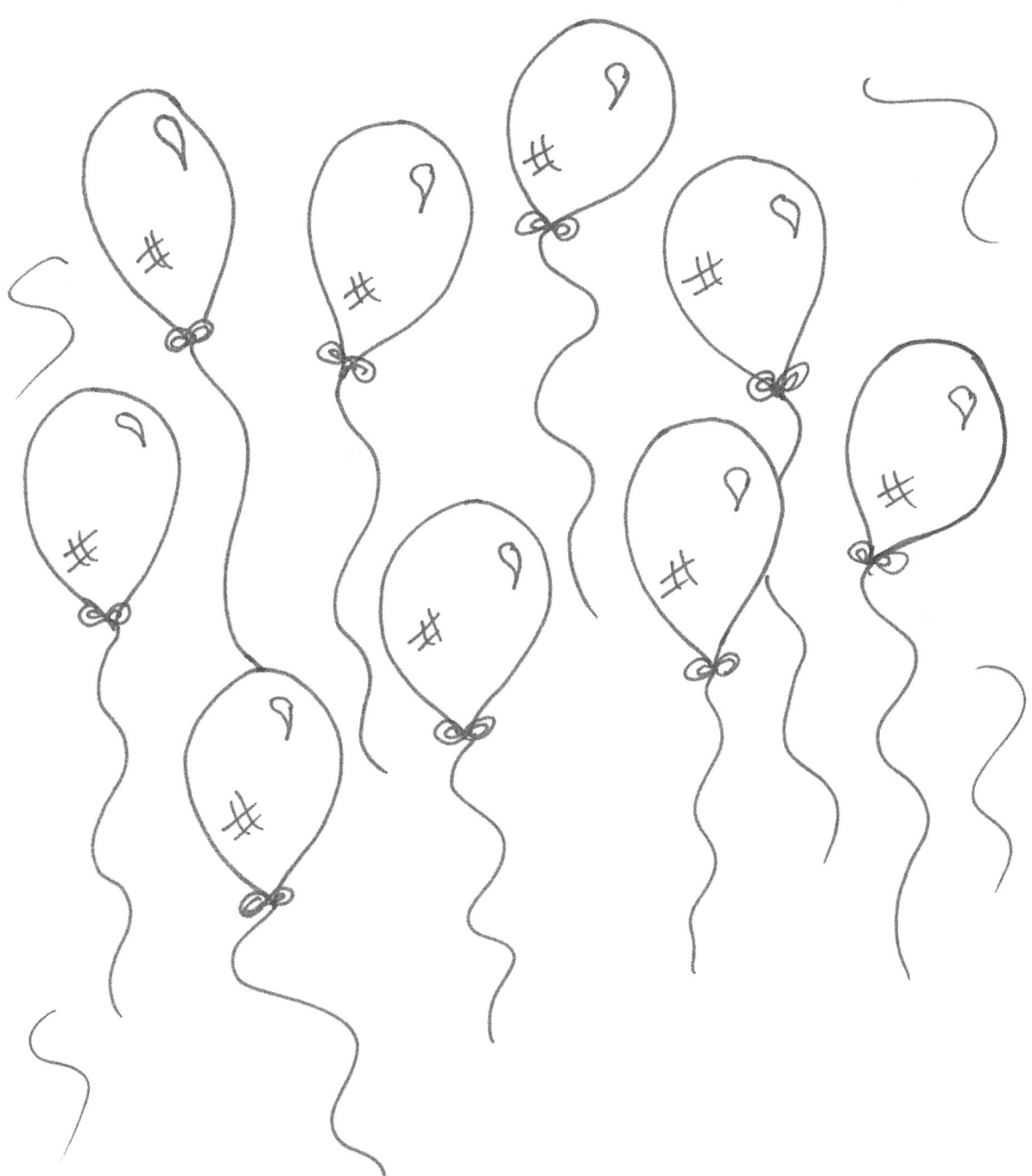

Sometimes it's Best to just Let It Go....

This page is a TEST or Doodle Page where you can Test and blend your colors before adding them to your coloring page. It also gives protection for any possible bleedthrough of pens, paints or markers.

Notes:

_____

_____

_____

_____

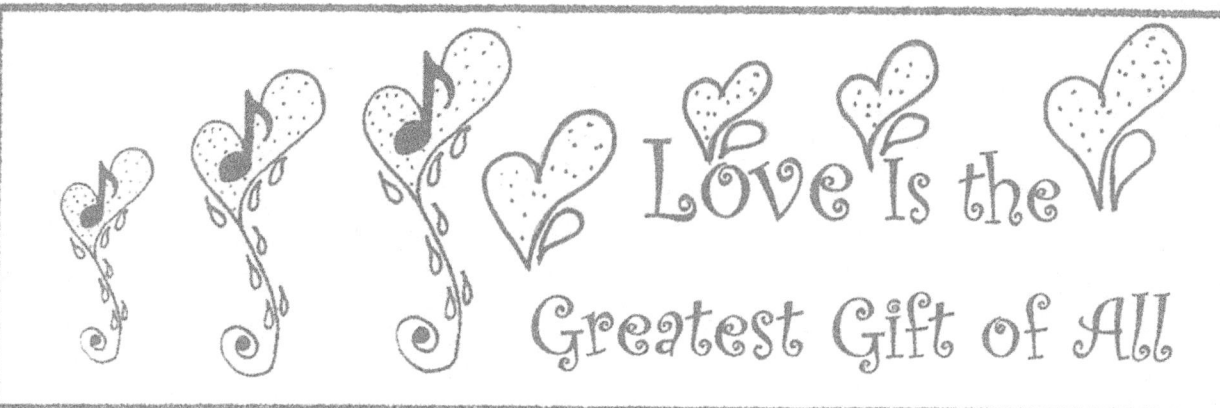

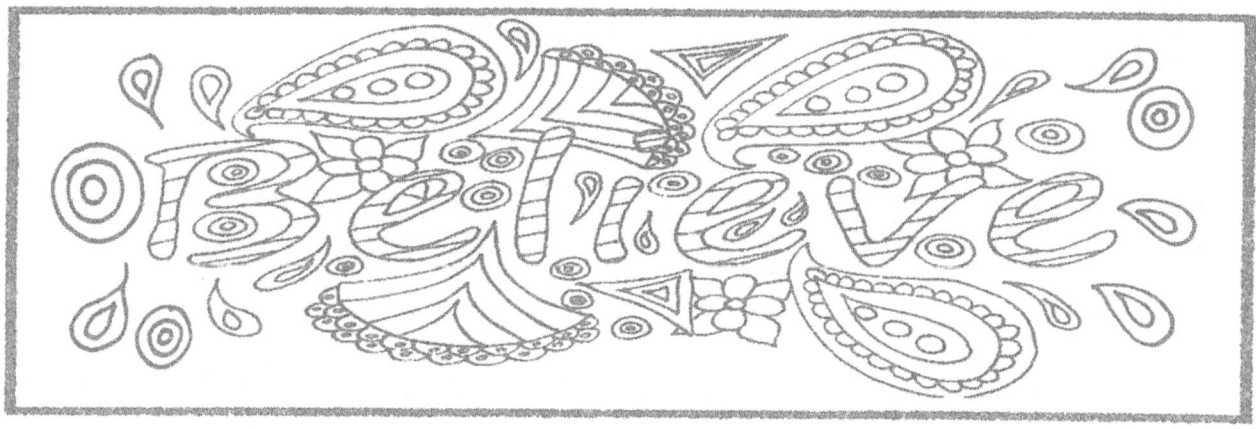

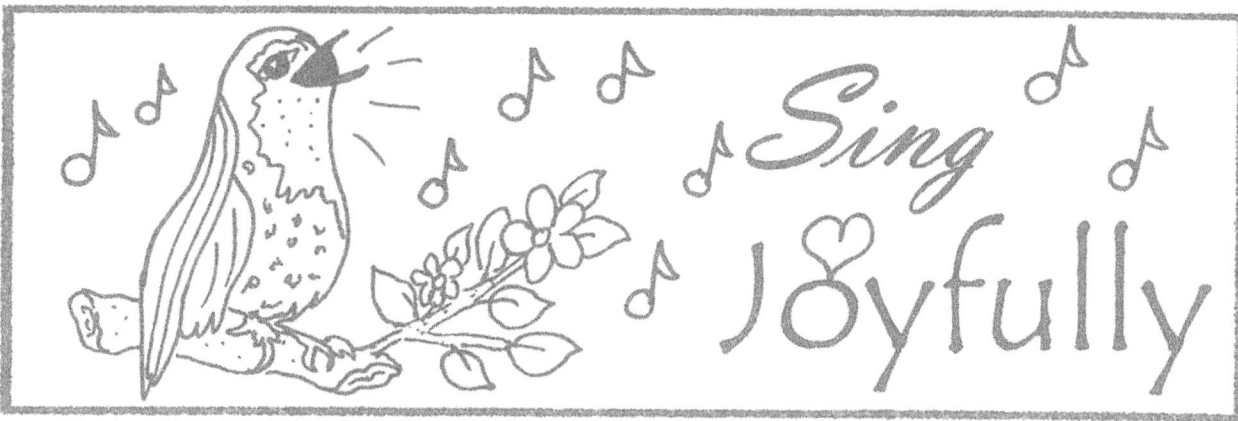

Bookmarks to Color~Cut out~

Give as Gifts or for your own use.

This page is a TEST or Doodle Page where you can Test and blend your colors before adding them to your coloring page. It also gives protection for any possible bleedthrough of pens, paints or markers.

Notes:

_____

_____

_____

_____

Bookmarks to CREATE Color~Cut out~
Give as Gifts or for your own use.

Color away All your
Troubles..

Find Joy in Each Day

Be Happy

Each Day is a Blessing and
a Fresh Start...